LOOKING BACK

CIVILIZATIONS OF PERU

BEFORE 1535

LOOKING BACK

CIVILIZATIONS OF PERU

BEFORE 1535

HAZEL MARY MARTELL

Austin, Texas

Editor: Nicola Barber, Pam Wells
Designer: Neil Sayer
Picture research: Victoria Brooker
Maps: Nick Hawken
Production: Jenny Mulvanny

Consultants: Dr. Cheryl Ann Sutherland, Department of Anthropology, University of Chicago; Dr Karen Wise, Assistant Curator, Department of Anthropology, Los Angeles County Museum of Natural History.

Library of Congress Cataloging-in-Publication Data

Martell, Hazel Mary.
Civilizations of Peru: before 1535 / Hazel Mary Martell.
p. cm. — (Looking back)
Includes bibliographical references (p. 62) and index.
Summary: An examination of several of the more important ancient civilizations of Peru with particular focus on the Incas and with attention drawn also to the effects of the Spanish conquests.
ISBN 0-8172-5428-5
1. Indians of South America — Peru — History — Juvenile literature. 2. Incas — Origin — Juvenile literature. 3. Incas — Social life and customs — Juvenile literature. 4. Peru — History — Conquest, 1522–1548 — Juvenile literature. [1. Indians of South America — Peru. 2. Incas. 3. Peru — History — Conquest, 1522–1548.] I. Title. II. Series.
F3429.M355 1999
985'.01 — dc21 98-20152
CIP AC

Printed in Spain
Bound in the United States
1 2 3 4 5 6 7 8 9 0 LB 02 01 00 99 98

Acknowledgments

Cover (main and background image) Tony Morrison/South American Pictures **title page** Robert Frerck/Robert Harding Picture Library **page 7** (top) Robert Harding Picture Library (bottom) Kimball Morrison/South American Pictures **page 8** H. R. Dörig/Hutchison Library **page 9** South American Pictures **page 10** Tony Morrison/South American Pictures **page 11** Walter Rawlings/Robert Harding Picture Library **page 12** e.t. archive **page 13** (top) e.t. archive (bottom) H. R. Dörig/Hutchison Library **page 14** Edward Parker/Hutchison Library **page 15** H. R. Dörig/Hutchison Library **page 17** George Rainbird Ltd/Robert Harding Picture Library **page 18** e.t. archive **page 19** Tony Morrison/South American Pictures **page 21** N. J Saunders/Werner Forman Archive **page 22** H. R. Dörig/Hutchison Library **page 23** Tony Morrison/South American Pictures **page 24** Tony Morrison/South American Pictures **page 25** Kimball Morrison/South American Pictures **page 27** Robert Frerck/Robert Harding Picture Library **page 28** (top) Hutchison Library (bottom) D. F. E. Russell/Robert Harding Picture Library **page 30** Werner Forman Archive **page 31** South American Pictures **page 32** Robert Harding Picture Library **page 33** South American Pictures **page 34** Tony Morrison/South American Pictures **page 36** Robert Harding Picture Library **page 37–39** Werner Forman **page 40** Tony Morrison/South American Pictures **page 41** H. R. Dörig/Hutchison Library **page 43** Tony Morrison/South American Pictures **page 45** (top) Tony Morrison/South American Pictures (bottom) Peter Ryley/South American Pictures **page 46** H. R. Dörig/Hutchison Library **page 47** (top) Werner Forman Archive (bottom) H. R. Dörig/Hutchison Library **page 48** Tony Morrison/South American Pictures **page 50–53** Werner Forman Archive **page 54** e.t. archive **page 57** South American Pictures **page 58** South American Pictures **page 59** Tony Morrison/South American Pictures

Contents

Introduction

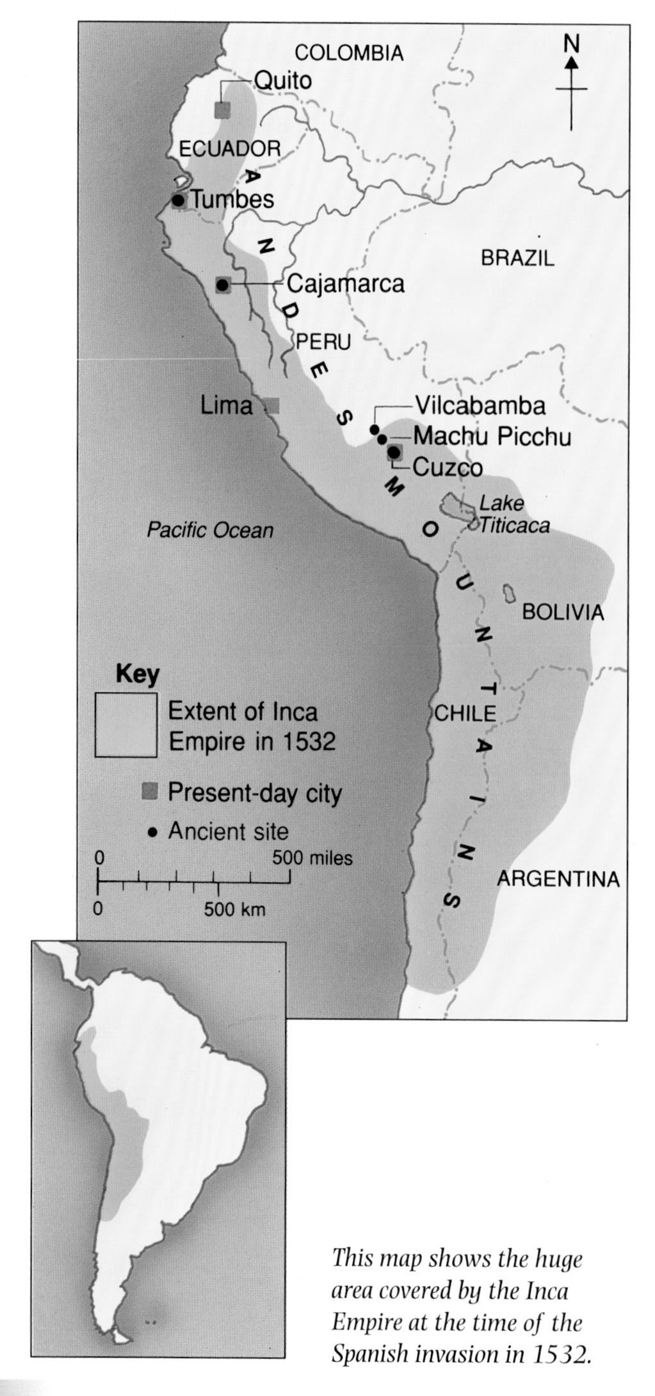

This map shows the huge area covered by the Inca Empire at the time of the Spanish invasion in 1532.

Although this book is about the ancient civilizations of Peru, it examines a much larger area in South America than the country we know as Peru today. It looks at the huge territory covered by the Inca Empire at the time of the Spanish invasion in 1532. This empire included parts of what are now Ecuador, Bolivia, Argentina, and Chile, in addition to modern-day Peru. Even in the centuries before the Incas gained control over the vast territories of their empire, these areas were linked by having similar cultures.

This region of South America is one of a startling variety of landscapes and climates. Along the Pacific coast runs a narrow strip of desert, dry and arid except where it is crossed by fertile river valleys. Rising dramatically from the desert are the Andes, some of the highest mountains in the world. Many of the highest peaks are permanently covered in snow and ice. Other features of these mountains include glaciers and volcanoes, while earthquakes and tremors often shake the area. In between the mountain ranges lie areas of high plain, known as *altiplano*. They are covered in bleak, treeless grassland, called *puna*. The lower slopes of the mountains are forested, especially on the eastern side where the rainfall is heaviest. To the east of the Andes lies the great Amazon basin, a vast area of tropical rain forest.

Today, the coastal desert of Peru is crossed from north to south by the Pan American Highway, but it is still a bleak and inhospitable area.

The valley of Callejon de Huaylas in the west of central Peru is overlooked by the Cordillera Blanca, a range of mountains containing some of the country's highest peaks.

The dry atmosphere of the coastal desert has helped to preserve artifacts such as this embroidered panel. Made by the Paracas people (see pages 16–18), it is part of a large piece of cloth that was wrapped around a dead person before burial.

A CLOSER LOOK

When the Spaniards arrived, the Incas spoke a language called Quechua. Because this language had never been written down, the Spaniards used their own spellings for the names of people and places, based on what they heard. However, there are now attempts to simplify the spellings of Inca words. This means that in some books you will see, for example, Inca written as Inka, Huari written as Wari, and Tiahuanaco written as Tiwanaku.

CIVILIZATIONS AND CONQUEST

Different cultures developed in this vast region at different times, and archaeologists recognize many civilizations in the 3,000-year period from 1400 B.C. to A.D. 1600. In chronological order, the most important are the Chavin, the Paracas, the Nazca, the Moche, the Tiahuanaco, the Huari, the Chimu, and finally, the Inca. They all have many things in common, especially in their arts and crafts, their gods, their architecture, their farming methods, and their trading patterns. Some, such as the Chimu and the Inca, developed independently at more or less the same time as each other, but none of them developed directly out of what had gone before. This book looks at each of these groups in turn, from the Chavin to the Inca. It also examines what happened to the Inca Empire and its people after 1532. At that time the Spanish conquistador, Francisco Pizarro and a small band of men arrived there looking for gold and other treasures.

HOW DO WE KNOW?

Most of our knowledge of Peru before 1535 comes from archaeological evidence, since none of the civilizations before that date had a system of writing. Even the archaeological evidence is not as rich as might be expected from civilizations that were flourishing as recently as 1530. This is because the Spanish conquistadores ransacked and destroyed many Inca towns and villages, seizing gold and silver objects to be melted down for bullion. They also destroyed any evidence of the Inca religion that they found, as they forced people to become Christians. In more recent times, grave-robbing has become a serious problem, as newly discovered graves are stripped of any treasure or other valuable artifacts. In spite of this, some things have survived remarkably well. These include the ruins of the ancient city of Machu Picchu, the tombs at Sipan, and the mysterious lines and pictures in the Nazca desert, all of which have been rediscovered in the 20th century. Scientific analysis of some of the surviving mummified bodies has revealed clues about what people died from, the diseases they suffered, and even something of what they ate and drank immediately before death.

Among Poma de Ayala's drawings of the Incas are some that illustrate the farming year. This one represents March and shows the guardian of the cornfield scaring away birds with a slingshot and a stick hung with bells.

There are also accounts of Inca life and customs written by Spanish priests and soldiers in the years immediately after the conquest. The drawings of the Incas made in the early 17th century by Poma de Ayala, who had an Inca mother and a Spanish father, are important, too. But neither of these may be entirely accurate, partly because they were based on other people's memories of what had happened in the past and partly because the Spaniards wrote from a European viewpoint that saw the Incas as backward and inferior to themselves.

From the First People to the Chavin

Like many of the rivers in Peru, the Ocona River flows west from the Andes Mountains to the coast. People in the river valleys along the coast were able to channel water to irrigate their fields.

The first people arrived in Peru between 12,000 and 10,000 years ago. They lived by hunting and gathering food from the wild, living in temporary shelters as they moved around in search of edible plants and animals. Two thousand years later, they were making their first attempts at cultivating some wild plants, including grasses, beans, peppers, and squash in the fertile valleys, but they still made their homes in temporary dwellings. By 6000 B.C. some grasses were being grown at higher altitudes, where potatoes were also being cultivated from the wild. It was only after about 3000 B.C., however, that the cultivation of plants was successful enough to allow people to settle permanently for longer periods in one place. Their earliest dwellings were cone-shaped huts, made from a framework of poles stuck into the ground in a circle, tied together at the top, and thatched with grass or reeds.

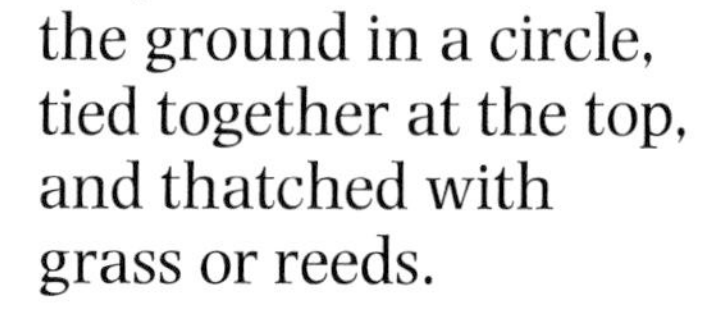

The first settlements

Once people had a more reliable source of food, the population expanded, and the first villages and towns began to develop. Between 4,000 and 5,000 years ago, villages appeared on the coast where fish, shellfish, and other sea creatures formed the daily diet. Around the same time, people also began to settle in the valleys of the rivers that crossed the desert between the mountains and the coast. There was very little rainfall in this area. However, the rivers flowed all year long since they were fed by streams in the mountains where rain was plentiful. Using this knowledge, the settlers developed simple irrigation systems that allowed them to grow the plants they had cultivated. They added to their diet by domesticating ducks for their meat, hunting wild birds, and catching fish from the rivers.

Around the same time, people were also beginning to settle down in the highlands. The main food crop was potatoes, while protein came from guinea pigs that were domesticated and eaten. However, the most important animals in the highlands were four different breeds of camelids, or animals that are related to camels. These were the vicuña, the guanaco, the llama, and the alpaca, all of which grazed on the large areas of *puna* between the mountain ranges. At first, all these animals were hunted for their meat. But by 2500 B.C. both llamas and alpacas had been domesticated, though the vicuña and the guanaco remained untamed.

Llamas still graze in the Andes today. These animals are in a pasture at around 13,100 feet (4,000 m) above sea level.

A CLOSER LOOK

Llamas and alpacas were very important to the farmers of Peru. Both animals provided meat and hides, as well as dung that could be dried and burned as fuel. They also provided wool. Llama wool was rough and strong and could be spun and used for ropes, blankets, and other heavy cloth. Alpaca wool was very fine and was woven to make warm clothing. Once they had been tamed, llamas were also used as transportation, carrying loads on their backs over the steep and narrow paths through the mountains. Some were also used in religious rituals and ceremonies (see page 42).

A gold model of a llama. It was made by the Incas as an offering to their gods.

TOWARD CIVILIZATIONS

A settled lifestyle and more reliable sources of food allowed an increasingly organized society to develop. By about 2300 B.C. people began to construct large-scale building projects. One of the earliest to be discovered so far is at Aspero, on the coast to the north of Lima, where, over several centuries, six rectangular platforms were built. These platforms rose up to a height of 33 feet (10 m) and were topped with stone buildings used for burials and religious purposes. Another temple, in the highlands of the Andes at La Galgada, was used for burials and for agricultural ceremonies. It was built of stone and mud around 2300 B.C., and its walls were plastered and painted. The tombs inside the temple contained the bodies of the local nobility, while ordinary people were buried outside the walls. This practice suggests that society was already forming into several, distinct social classes.

From items left in these and other temples and tombs, we know that people in these settlements traded goods over a large area. They obtained cotton and colored shells from the people on the coast, and wool and root crops from people in the highlands. They traded for colored feathers and a hallucinogenic powder from the people in the rain forests to the east of the Andes. By 2000 B.C. they

This pottery jar from the Moche civilization (see pages 20–22) shows a woman wearing a headdress made from corncobs. She might be a goddess.

had added corn to the list of crops they cultivated. They had also begun to make pottery vessels to replace the plant gourds previously used for both storing and cooking food.

From around 1700 B.C., people began to build much larger ceremonial centers. These were also on mounds and usually had a U-shaped temple as their most important structure. Their size suggests that they were built by people from more than one village, which, in turn, suggests that a new sort of society was beginning to develop, paving the way for the first complex civilization.

THE CHAVIN CIVILIZATION

The first well-developed civilization in Peru was the Chavin. Its name is taken from a site called Chavin de Huantar, a temple complex that thrived 10,500 feet (3,200 m) up in the northern highlands of Peru between about 850 and 200 B.C. The Chavin culture began to develop around 900 B.C. and, at its height around 500 B.C., its influence spread throughout most of northern and central Peru and along much of the south coast. Nobody knows for certain, but it seems unlikely that all these places were united

A CLOSER LOOK

Some of what we know as dangerous drugs today were widely used by the Incas and their predecessors. Priests and shamans often took a hallucinogenic drug to help them in their religious ceremonies and to predict the future. Many other people chewed the leaves of the coca plant as part of their everyday lives. It is thought that this helped them to cope with the problems of tiredness and hunger that are a result of living at a high altitude.

Though most people have a serious concern about this use, coca leaves are still chewed in Peru today

politically under one ruler. Instead they were linked by their religion, which archaeologists have learned much about from the remains at Chavin de Huantar.

The temple complex

Chavin de Huantar stands on one of the few passes through the Andes that remains snow-free all year. The oldest part of its temple complex is a U-shaped structure, with its open end facing east. It is built on top of platforms of stone rubble, faced with smooth stone. Inside these platforms are several rooms and galleries, including one containing pottery vessels that were brought from different parts of Peru to Chavin de Huantar, suggesting that it was a place of pilgrimage. Most of the vessels at the site were broken, but the bones of guinea pigs, fish, llamas, and deer found among the pieces of pottery suggest that they once contained food offerings.

Many of the images found in and around the temple at Chavin de Huantar have fierce, snarling faces. This one also carries severed heads on its belt, as trophies of victories over its enemies.

Images of the gods

The temple complex at Chavin de Huantar was built of huge blocks of stone, including white granite and black andesite, on which there are carved images of many different gods. Archaeologists believe that three of these images were more important than the others, either because their images are bigger or because they have also been found in later civilizations. No one knows their original names, but archaeologists have called the first one the Great Image, the Smiling God, or El Lanzón, meaning "the lance." It has long fangs, a snarling expression, and

A CLOSER LOOK
Many of the Chavin temples contained oracles through which the gods "spoke" to the people. It is thought that the effect was achieved by a hidden priest talking through a trumpet made from a conch shell. These shells were found on the coast of Ecuador and were traded along the length of the Andes.

hair like snakes, and is carved into a narrow piece of rock that is 15 feet (4.5 m) tall. The second is the Staff God, which has a human body but a catlike face and holds a staff in either hand. (See page 38.) Both of these are in the temple, but the third one is in a courtyard and is the image of a caiman carved into an oblong pillar. Other carvings on the walls at Chavin include jaguars, eagles, snakes, and parrots. These, together with images of the Staff God, continue to appear in various forms on stone carvings, pottery, textiles, and gold and silver objects through to Inca times.

A twin-handled pot, known as a stirrup pot, made in Chavin de Huantar. It is decorated with the image of the Smiling God.

EVERYDAY LIFE

Archaeologists believe that Chavin de Huantar grew from a settlement of around 500 farmers and herders in 850 B.C. to a town of around 2,000 to 3,000 people by 250 B.C. Its most important inhabitants lived in tall, stone houses, built on wide terraces surrounding the temple complex, and separate from the rest of the population. They ate meat from young llamas and wore jewelry, including rings, ear disks, and pendants made from gold. Most other towns of the period grew up separately from the temple complexes. In addition to farmers, herders, and traders, the inhabitants included people who were not directly involved in the production of food, such as goldsmiths, silversmiths, potters, stone carvers, and textile workers.

The Paracas, Nazca, and Moche

During the 3rd century B.C. the Chavin civilization began to collapse, but with no written records, no one today can be sure why this happened. One possibility is that the various communities began to develop in different ways, and, without the firm structure of a state to hold them together, they gradually drifted apart. The ceremonial centers were abandoned, and at Chavin de Huantar farmers used some of the carved stones from the temple to build the walls of their houses. Several centuries would pass before another distinct civilization developed in the highlands, but in this same period archaeologists have identified various civilizations on the coast and in the short river valleys that cross the desert.

The Paracas civilization

The oldest civilization on the coast of Peru is that of the Paracas, which probably began to develop before 600 B.C., when the Chavin was still flourishing, and lasted until about A.D. 175. One of the most extraordinary sites of the Paracas civilization was the windswept, treeless Paracas peninsula that juts out into the Pacific Ocean between the valleys of the Pisco and Ica rivers. This peninsula seems to have been a ritual center, and a number of cemeteries complete with mummified bodies have been discovered there. However, the people of the Paracas civilization lived north of this peninsula, in river valleys near the coast.

Much of the information about

A closer look

The name Paracas comes from a Quechuan word that means "sand falling like rain" and is used to describe the sandstorms that start abruptly on the peninsula toward the end of each afternoon and die away just as abruptly at dusk.

the Paracas civilization has come from archaeological excavations. The dry climate of this area has helped to preserve the remains of food and artifacts, such as textiles and featherwork that would have rotted away in damper places. The excavation of various settlement sites has showed that the Paracas people ate corn, peanuts, and cassava and got most of their protein from fish. They also made baskets and used plant gourds for containers.

However, the cemeteries were even more revealing. This is because the bodies buried in them were not only mummified but also wrapped up in bundles of cloth, most of which contained grave goods of various kinds.

A mummy bundle from one of the cemeteries on the Paracas peninsula. Underneath all the wrappings the bodies were naked and mummified naturally in the hot sand.

Unlike Ancient Egyptian mummies that had their limbs straightened out, Paracas mummies were usually in a sitting position with their knees tucked up toward their chins. They were enclosed in a piece of plain, cotton cloth. Ordinary people were buried like this, but more prominent people were placed inside a large, shallow basket that was then wrapped around with more layers of cloth until it made a large, cone-shaped bundle. Some of the layers of cloth were plain, but others were richly patterned with panels of embroidery, showing images of plants and animals, humans, gods, and mythical creatures. Some of these were similar to those used by the Chavin people.

Many of the bundles contained intricately woven and embroidered clothing, such as skirts and tunics, mantles, loincloths, and *ruanas* (ponchos), as well as headbands made from fur and feathers. Some also had simple gold ornaments tucked between the layers of cloth or in the mouth of the mummy. Others were surrounded by pottery objects, especially bowls and

A CLOSER LOOK

Grave goods and other artifacts in the Paracas cemeteries show that this civilization was wealthy. The Paracas people imported raw materials, such as wool from the highlands, feathers from the rain forests, and shells from the north coast. No one can be certain of what was traded in exchange, but some possibilities are sea salt and salted fish.

bottles with double spouts joined by a handle. It seems likely that the embroidery on the burial cloths related to the person's *ayllu*, or social group ties. (See pp. 51–52.) But not enough is known about the Paracas religion to decide whether the other objects were meant to be used in another life, or were gifts for the gods.

This pottery figure of a seated woman is from the Nazca civilization. No one knows whether the marks under her eyes are spots or tattoos.

THE NAZCA CIVILIZATION

Around the time that the Chavin civilization was collapsing, another new civilization was developing in the river valleys on the southern coast of Peru. Named Nazca after the valley on which it was centered, its influence spread north and south to include the Pisco, Chincha, Ica, Palpo, and Acari valleys. Its people lived mainly by farming, developing underground irrigation channels, called *pukios*, to make it possible to grow large crops of corn, beans, and peppers in the harsh, desert climate. Their textiles and pottery shared similarities with those of the nearby Paracas people. Later they developed their own distinctive styles, especially in pottery where four or more colors were often used in painted designs featuring people, plants, birds, fish, and animals. Some were realistic, but others were mythical creatures and demons with lengthened features. Toward the end of the Nazca period, images of trophy heads—heads that were cut from the bodies of defeated enemies and taken as trophies or prizes—were used in designs on both textiles and pottery. Mummified human heads, probably from prisoners taken in combat, have also been found at some Nazca sites. It is thought that these heads were used in religious ceremonies to ensure good harvests.

The main center of the Nazca religion was at Cahuachi in the Nazca Valley where platform mounds and huge adobe pyramids, separated by courts and plazas, were built over a period of about 700 years. The largest construction is the Great Temple, which is a stepped pyramid almost 65 feet (20 m) high. Thousands of people were buried in cemeteries surrounding Cahuachi. Like the Paracas people, they were placed in a sitting position, wrapped in cloth, and given grave goods that included pottery and ornaments made from hammered gold.

However, the most spectacular and puzzling remains of the Nazca civilization are the so-called Nazca Lines on the surface of the desert next to the Nazca Valley. These include straight lines and geometric shapes, as well as enormous drawings of

The spider was the first figure to be recognized by María Reiche (see page 20) when she began studying the Nazca Lines in 1946. Like the rest of the lines, it survived through the centuries because the extreme dryness of the area prevented plants and grasses growing over it.

A CLOSER LOOK

After the collapse of the Nazca civilization, in the 8th century A.D., the Nazca Lines went unnoticed until the 1920s, when they were thought to be ancient roads crossing the desert. Their true significance was not rediscovered until the 1940s when the German archaeologist, María Reiche, began to examine them. She studied them for many decades, often from a high ladder, and concluded that they were used for the science of astronomy.

plants and animals. They were made by removing the small stones that cover the surface of the desert to reveal the light-colored soil underneath. The animals represented by the lines include a monkey, a killer whale, a spider, and a hummingbird, while the geometric shapes include triangles and trapezoids.

There are many different theories as to why they were created. Some people think they tie in with solar or astronomical observations. There is evidence that the Nazca used hot-air balloons to view the lines from above. María Reiche had found that the lines pointed to the Sun, Moon, and the stars on important dates in astronomy. Others think they point to sacred places in the mountains or relate to the irrigation systems. Another theory is that they were offerings to the gods, made in times of extreme drought or other disasters. These lines might also have been created as pathways for religious processions.

THE MOCHE CIVILIZATION

While the Paracas and Nazca civilizations flourished in the coastal region of southern Peru, the Moche (or Mochica) civilization developed on the northern coast. Starting around A.D. 1, it lasted to around A.D. 800. Its name is taken from the site of Moche in the valley of the Moche River. From there its influence spread over 217 miles (350 km) between the Lambayeque Valley in the north and the Nepena Valley in the south.

Like the Paracas and Nazca people, the Moche built an extensive irrigation system that enabled them to grow large crops of corn, beans, peppers, peanuts, and sweet potatoes in the rainless valleys. They also built urban centers, the most important of which was Moche itself, near the present-day town

A CLOSER LOOK

The Pyramid of the Sun is a stepped pyramid, measuring 1,115 feet (340 m) by 446 feet (136 m) at its base, and standing 135 feet (41 m) high. Estimates suggest that over 125 million adobe bricks were used to build it. At the time of its construction, it was probably the largest structure in the Americas.

of Trujillo. The settlement there is dominated by two huge structures, known as the Pyramid of the Sun and the Pyramid of the Moon, surrounded by evidence of a densely populated city.

The two large pyramids at Moche were religious and ceremonial centers, but many other pyramids in the region were the tombs of an elite class of warrior-priests. Most of the pyramids have been robbed over the centuries, but in 1987 archaeologists were able to excavate one that was almost intact at Huaca Rajada, near Sipan in the Lambayeque Valley. An outer tomb in the pyramid had been ransacked by grave-robbers, but an inner tomb contained an undisturbed wooden coffin with gold and feather headdresses, clothing decorated with gold, silver, and copper, banners, shell beads, and gold and silver jewelry decorated with precious stones. They also found the body of a man who had been about 40 years old when he died in around

A reconstruction of the Royal Tomb at Sipan. The man known as the Lord of Sipan was buried in the large coffin in the center.

A.D. 300. Nicknamed the Lord of Sipan, he was buried with two men and three women, all in separate coffins, plus a third man who had been buried without a coffin and with his feet cut off, probably to prevent his running away. In addition to its beautiful artifacts, this discovery has added to archaeologists' knowledge of the Moche civilization by showing that its influence extended far beyond the Moche Valley, while the number and status of the people in the tomb are further evidence of the complexity of Moche society.

Apart from the tomb of the Lord of Sipan, the Moche civilization is probably most famous for its pottery. Many Moche vessels were painted with scenes from everyday life or with scenes of religious or political rituals. Others were modeled into the shape of people or animals and depict many aspects of everyday life. Some jars are in the shape of human faces, often with such realistic features that they very well may have been portraits of actual people. Many pots also show warriors and aspects of the warfare that probably helped the Moche civilization to expand as far as it did.

This stirrup pot is in the shape of a Moche chief. It was filled or emptied through the spout which is in the middle of the looped, hollow handle behind the head.

Despite its wealth, the Moche civilization collapsed around A.D. 800. There are several possible reasons: a succession of natural disasters such as earthquakes, prolonged drought, sand dunes drifting on to populated areas, or even flooding caused by the climatic condition known as El Niño.

The Tiahuanaco, Huari, and Chimu

Lake Titicaca lies high in the Andes Mountains. Today, the Uru people continue to make boats from bundles of dried totora reeds, just as the people of Tiahuanaco did over 1,500 years ago.

Following the collapse of the Chavin, there was no unifying civilization in the highlands for several centuries. People carried on farming and trading, making textiles and pottery, but they lived in individual communities with very little influence beyond their own immediate area. Eventually, however, some communities in the highlands around Lake Titicaca, in what is now Bolivia, became more powerful and developed into small city-states, of which the best-known are Pucara and Chiripa. The area of influence of these city-states was limited, but they were followed by others that became powerful enough to start the unification of the peoples of the highlands once more. The first civilization to develop in this way was Tiahuanaco near the southern shore of Lake Titicaca.

The Tiahuanaco civilization

People began to settle in the area of Tiahuanaco around 1000 B.C., but construction of the temple complex, the ruins of which can be seen today, was probably started around the first century A.D. The civilization itself did not begin to expand outside the Titicaca basin until around A.D. 500.

At an altitude of 12,000 feet (3,660 m) above sea level, Tiahuanaco was the highest ancient city in the Andes. It was also in one of the bleakest landscapes. Situated on the *altiplano*, the treeless *puna* provides

The huge Ponce monolith, or great stone, represents one of the many gods worshiped at Tiahuanaco.

no shelter from the biting winds. In spite of this, its farmers were able to grow enough food to feed as many as 50,000 people living in the city center at its height. They did this by means of the raised-field system that reclaimed land from the marshy areas near the shore of the lake.

Crops were planted in special prepared platforms measuring between 13 and 30 feet (4 to 9 m) wide and between 30 to 295 feet (9 to 90 m) long. The platforms stood about 3 feet (1 m) above the surrounding area, and the extra soil needed to make them was taken from the channels dug out around them. Then, the channels were filled with water that absorbed the sun's heat during the day and released it as mist at night when the air temperature fell sharply.

This system protected the plants from frost damage and also extended the growing season. The algae and water plants in the canals attracted ducks and birds and were later dug out and used as fertilizers on the fields. This way they could produce two crops each year.

The abundance of food produced by the raised-field system meant that not everybody had to work on the land in order to eat. In turn, this allowed Tiahuanaco to develop into a ceremonial and religious center with many fine structures made from massive stone blocks that were imported from across Lake Titicaca. These structures include the Akapana Pyramid, a stepped platform made from earth and faced with cut stone that had several temples on the top, a partially underground temple with stone heads fixed into the walls, and a low, oblong platform called the Kalasasaya. In one corner of the Kalasasaya there is

A CLOSER LOOK

Archaeologists believe that the influence of the civilization of Tiahuanaco spread through trade and a shared religion, rather than through warfare and conquest. No evidence of fortifications or weapons has been found. These scientists think that the city of Tiahuanaco was a center of pilgrimage. People traveled great distances to the city to see the stone carvings, some of which were on pillars up to 23 feet (7 m) in height.

a huge doorway, sometimes called the Gateway of the Sun, which is cut from a single block of basalt, a type of volcanic rock. A figure carved over the center of the doorway looks like the Staff God of the Chavin civilization. It is flanked on either side by three rows of carved, winged figures. Archaeologists have nicknamed this figure the Gateway God. His image and that of the winged figures are found on stone carvings and pottery throughout the whole area influenced by Tiahuanaco.

The civilization of Tiahuanaco reached its greatest extent between about A.D. 500 and 1000. During this time its influence covered large parts of what are now south and east Bolivia, southern Peru,

The Gateway of the Sun is one of the few ancient structures to have survived at Tiahuanaco.

This map shows the main places mentioned in this chapter and the two previous ones.

northern Chile, and the northwest of Argentina. But despite this success, Tiahuanaco declined in the 10th century A.D., possibly as the result of a prolonged drought that made it impossible to grow enough food to feed its people. Its inhabitants spread widely throughout the mountains and valleys of the southern Andes.

THE HUARI CIVILIZATION

The Huari civilization began to develop around A.D. 600 in the central highlands of Peru. It is named after the town of Huari, which is at its center. Its people cut terraces in the steep hillsides to make flat areas on which they could grow crops. (You can read more about this on page 43.) Apart from this, it had much in common with Tiahuanaco, including the images of the Gateway God and his attendants that are found on Huari textiles, pottery, stone carvings, and artifacts in gold and copper. However, no one knows exactly how, or even if, the two civilizations were connected to each other.

A CLOSER LOOK

The Huari built administrative centers throughout their empire. One of these was at Pikillacta, around 19 miles (30 km) from where the Incas would later build their capital, Cuzco. Pikillacta was built to a square grid pattern and contained over 700 buildings, some of which were three stories high. The walls of the buildings were of rough stone, set in a cement made from mud, and plastered over with coats of clay to make them smooth. This was in contrast to the buildings at Tiahuanaco. Those were constructed from massive stone blocks, cut, and shaped so carefully that no mortar was needed to hold them together.

By A.D. 800 the Huari sphere of influence stretched north as far as the Cajamara and Chicama valleys and south as far as the Ocona Valley. It seems to have been run as an empire, with palaces and rich tombs in Huari suggesting there was a distinct ruling class. Large-scale storage facilities and evidence of recordkeeping in the town suggest that some sort of tribute was paid as taxes. However, there are conflicting views about how its influence spread. Some people believe that the empire expanded through military conquest, but others think that its expansion was through trade and the spread of a shared religion. The Huari empire reached its greatest extent around A.D. 800. Then for some unknown reason people began to abandon the city of Huari, and the civilization started to collapse. By around A.D. 900 Huari itself had been abandoned, and many people in the highlands had gone back to living in small rural communities rather than in large urban centers.

The skills of Chimu goldsmiths can be seen in this figure which is part of the hilt of a ceremonial knife, or tumi.

THE CHIMU CIVILIZATION

Following the collapse of the Huari and Tiahuanaco civilizations, Peru was once more divided into small, independent states, most of which were confined to their own river valleys. One of these states was that of the Chimu in the Moche Valley on the north coast of Peru. The Chimu inhabited this valley by about A.D. 1000, although initial settlement was probably as early as A.D. 800. Like all the people before them, they irrigated the dry land and grew corn and other crops to feed themselves. They were skilled at weaving, featherwork, and making pottery. Chimu metalworkers

A CLOSER LOOK

Today, the ruins of Chan Chan cover an area of around 10 square miles (25 sq km). They are well preserved because so little rain falls in the area. The city is divided into rectangular blocks of buildings separated by streets. At its center there are about ten large enclosures, known as *ciudadelas*, or citadels, surrounded by adobe and rammed earth walls that are about 10 feet (3 m) wide at their base and about 30 feet (9 m) high. It is thought that these citadels were palaces and that a new one was built for each successive ruler, while the old ones were sealed up. Each *ciudadela* had just one door leading from the outside into a large courtyard. Beyond this was a complex of storerooms and courtyards, probably used for storing and distributing goods that had been obtained as tax or tribute. The royal living quarters were along one side of the *ciudadela* and, after death, the ruler was buried within the *ciudadela* with his worldly possessions.

Details of a frieze at Chan Chan (right) and the ruins of one of the ciudadelas *(below).*

also produced magnificent artifacts in gold, silver, and copper that were often decorated with a mosaic pattern of semiprecious stones, such as turquoise. Around A.D. 1200 the Chimu started to build their capital city, Chan Chan. (See page 28.) Early in the following century, as their population grew, they began to expand the territory under their control by means of conquest.

THE CHIMU EMPIRE AND SOCIETY

By 1450 the Chimu controlled an empire that stretched along the coast from Piura in the north almost to present-day Lima in the south. The empire was run from Chan Chan, and roads were constructed to make trade and communication easier. Cities were also built in other parts of the empire. These cities were similar in layout to Chan Chan and probably served as local centers of administration, where taxes and tribute could be collected and distributed. Society was divided into distinct classes, with peasants and farmers at the bottom and a powerful aristocracy at the top, led by a ruler who was probably thought to be a god. In the middle were craftworkers, many of whom were highly respected.

THE DECLINE OF THE CHIMU

Although Chimu was a powerful and well-organized state, it was conquered by the Incas in 1476. One possible reason for this is that it depended on its irrigation systems to feed its population. If these failed, people went hungry. Oral tradition says that the Incas realized this and stopped the supply of water to the canals around Chan Chan. However, another tradition says that the Chimu decided that the Incas' weapons were too powerful for them to resist. Another possibility is that the cost of maintaining all the unused palaces in Chan Chan (see page 28) used up wealth that should have gone into strengthening the empire. This made it easier for the Incas to gain control and make the Chimu lands part of their own empire.

The Rise of the Incas

The last widespread civilization to develop in Peru before 1535 was that of the Incas. According to tradition, the rise of the Incas started toward the end of the 12th century A.D. At this time the highlands of Peru were once more divided into many different communities, following the collapse of the Tiahuanaco and Huari civilizations. Like all the earlier civilizations in South America, the Incas had no written language, so the story of their origins was passed down by word of mouth from one generation to the next. It was eventually written down by the Spaniards, but by that time nobody knew for certain what was fact and what was myth.

Inca origins

Inca tradition says that the Inca civilization started around A.D. 1200, when Manco Capac decided to move his people about 16 miles (25 km) north from the village of

A closer look

Although the Incas had no system of writing, specially trained officials kept records on lengths of knotted string, known as *quipus* (left). The position and size of a knot related to the number it represented. For example, a simple knot stood for one, while longer knots stood for numbers up to nine. A knot with three loops at the bottom of the string was three, but if it was farther up it represented 30. Farther up still it was 300 and at the top of the string it was 3,000 or 30,000. Different colored strings related to the different things that were being counted.

A CLOSER LOOK
The people we call Incas called themselves Quechua, which is also the name given to the language they spoke. In this language, the word *Inca* means "lord" and was the word they used to describe their leader. When the Spaniards took control of the Inca Empire in the 16th century, they used the word *Inca* to describe all the people living in the empire. In reality, the empire was made up of many different peoples who spoke at least 20 different languages.

Paqari-tampu to the site of present-day Cuzco. Today, no one knows whether Manco Capac was a real or a legendary leader, or why he decided to move his people when he did. He might have been looking for better farming land. One legend relates that he and his sister, Mama Huaca, took with them a magic, golden rod that had been given to them by Inti, the Sun god. Inti told them to settle at the place where they could push the rod deep into the ground, because the soil would be good and fertile for growing crops. They kept trying and finally succeeded at the place that became their capital, Cuzco.

TOWARD AN EMPIRE

During the 200 years after they settled in Cuzco, the Incas gradually grew more powerful. They attacked and defeated neighboring communities in the Cuzco Valley, but they did not attempt to take control of them. Instead, the Incas forced the defeated peoples to pay tribute (tax) in exchange for their freedom. In the 14th century, the Incas made their first conquests of lands outside the Cuzco Valley. Again this was only on a small scale, and no Inca officials were sent to rule over the defeated peoples. Then, in 1438 a new ruler came to the Inca throne. His name was Pachacuti Inca Yupanqui, and he claimed to be a direct descendant of the gods of Tiahuanaco. In addition to being ambitious, he was also a military genius. He set out to conquer the neighboring lands by force and make them all part of an Inca Empire.

The Emperor Pachacuti, as drawn by Poma de Ayala in about 1620.

A TIME OF RAPID EXPANSION

In less than 100 years from the start of Pachacuti's rule, the Incas expanded the territory under their control until they had an empire that stretched for over 2,175 miles (3,500 km) from north to south and an average of 200 miles (320 km) from east to west. The empire had a population of between ten and twelve million people. This expansion was achieved by the determination of just three rulers. Between 1438 and 1463 Pachacuti and his army conquered the central highlands to the west of Cuzco. He then turned his attention to ruling his expanding empire and handed the task of further conquest on to his son, Topa Inca.

While Pachacuti was still alive, Topa Inca conquered the Chimu lands. He also tried to invade the Amazon rain forest but was unsuccessful because his army

The Inca fortress of Sacsahuamán overlooks Cuzco. It is said that 20,000 people worked on the construction of this fortress. Some stones are over 20 feet (6 m) tall and weigh more than 100 tons.

A CLOSER LOOK

The Inca soldier's main weapon was a short wooden club, tipped with either stone or bronze. He wore a wooden helmet to protect his head and carried a wooden shield to protect his body. He also carried a slingshot that he used to hurl stones at the enemy at the start of a battle. This was a skill he practiced from childhood when he was sent to kill the birds that came to feed on the growing crops. Most of the soldiers were farmers who only served in the army for a certain length of time as a way of paying their *mit'a* or tax paid with manual labor. (See page 35.)

According to Poma de Ayala, Inca generals were carried into battle by four men.

found it difficult to fight in the dense vegetation. When he became Sapa Inca (meaning Sole Ruler) in 1471, Topa headed south to conquer the southern highlands and coastal areas. However, when he reached the center of present-day Chile, he met strong resistance from the Araucanian people, and after a fierce battle, he decided to make this the southern boundary of the Inca Empire.

After Topa's death in 1493, his son Huayna Capac became the next Sapa Inca. He added parts of the northern highlands and coastal areas as far as present-day Quito to the empire. But before he could go any farther, he was taken ill and died in 1525.

CONTROLLING THE EMPIRE

As his empire grew ever larger, Pachacuti devised ways of ruling it from his capital, Cuzco. He employed thousands of officials who worked throughout the empire. He also set up a network of roads to provide access between Cuzco and the rest of the empire. This network allowed the army to move quickly to any part of the empire. It meant that vital supplies such as food and other goods could be transported

The ruins of Tambo Colorado, one of the resting-places for Inca messengers, can still be seen in the coastal desert of Peru today.

COREON·MAJOR·I MENOR
HATVN CHASQVI CHVRI
MVLLO·CHASQVI·CVRACA

easily. The roads were vital for communication, too. The emperor sent and received orders and information from all corners of the empire by means of official messengers. These messengers lived in huts that were 1.2 miles (2 km) apart on every road. They memorized each message, then ran with it to the next hut to pass it on. In this way, information could travel up to 155 miles (250 km) in a single day.

Pachacuti and later emperors also kept control of the Inca lands by building new towns in the conquered territories and sending teachers to the subject peoples to show them the Inca way of life. Those who accepted this way of life were usually allowed to remain in their own communities, but

As an Inca messenger approached a hut, he blew into a conch-shell horn to alert the next messenger.

A CLOSER LOOK
The Incas called their empire Tahuantisuyu, which means "The Land of the Four Quarters." This was because the empire was divided into four provinces, or *suyus*, each representing one of the four main points of the compass, with Cuzco at the center. Each province was further divided into smaller units, made up of a number of *ayllus*, or communities. The Inca rulers made everyone wear the special clothing of their village or *ayllu*, so that they were easily identifiable.

groups from rebellious communities were sometimes moved to distant parts of the empire. They were replaced in the community by groups of more loyal people who would report any wrongdoings to the Inca rulers. This policy was intended to discourage any large-scale rebellion against the Incas.

TAXES

The Incas kept their empire running by taxing people in two different ways. Each community used about one-third of its land to grow crops for the Inca, and another third to grow crops for the gods, while the rest was used to grow crops for themselves. People also produced a certain amount of textiles for the Inca each year. On top of this there was a labor tax, known as *mit'a*, that all able-bodied men between the ages of about 16 and 60 had to pay by working for the empire for a period of time each year. This work included serving in the army, building roads, working on irrigation and drainage projects, constructing terraces for agriculture, quarrying stone, mining gold, and helping to build new towns and fortresses. In return, the Inca rulers made sure that everyone was fed and clothed, even in times of poor harvests. Many of the crops dedicated to the gods were returned to the people during religious feasts and ceremonies.

A CLOSER LOOK
***Quipus* (see page 30) were used to keep a historical record of the goods provided by each *ayllu* for the Sapa Inca, the number of people living in each household, and how many households there were in each *ayllu*. Unfortunately, most of the *quipus* were destroyed by the Spaniards who thought they were the work of the devil, so the skill of using them was lost. Some still survive, but none of them can be understood today.**

Inca Society and Everyday Life

A closer look
Legend says that the first Incas were Manco Capac, his three brothers, and four sisters. They emerged from the middle cave of three at Paqari-tampu. Manco Capac married Mama Huaca, who was one of his sisters, and they had a son. This son, Sinchi Roca, became Sapa Inca when Manco Capac died. After that, although the Sapa Inca was allowed to have many wives, at least one of them had to be his sister, known as the Coya, to provide an heir. Like the Sapa Inca himself, the Coya was thought to be a child of the Sun. By marrying her, the Sapa Inca ensured that his heir would also be descended directly from the Sun.

The success of the Incas depended on two main factors. The first was their ability to adopt and adapt some of the best features of the earlier civilizations in Peru. The second factor was their skill in organizing their society so that everyone knew their place in it and what was expected of them.

The social structure

Inca society was like an enormous pyramid with the Sapa Inca at the top and nobles, who were mainly his relatives, just below him. At first, only these nobles were permitted to help the Sapa Inca with the process of government. But as the empire expanded there were not enough Inca nobles to oversee all of it. So the Sapa Inca granted privileges to groups close, and loyal, to Cuzco. Later, the Incas allowed cooperative chiefs of conquered lands to continue governing their own territories. These chiefs and their families made up a new class of people, known as the *curacas.* Like the Inca nobles, they did not have to pay any taxes. To make absolutely certain that these chiefs

This featherwork fan was used by one of the Sapa Inca's slaves to flick the flies from the ruler's face.

stayed loyal to the Sapa Inca, their sons were taken to Cuzco as hostages, where they learned how to live and rule according to Inca ways.

Below the *curacas* was a group of less important officials, known as the *camayoq*. Each one was responsible for a certain number of peasant households. Finally, at the bottom of the pyramid came the millions of peasants. They grew the food and paid the taxes that kept the vast Inca Empire running. The whole Inca society was divided up into groups, called *ayllus*. (See page 35.) Members of an *ayllu* shared common ancestors and worshiped at the same *huacas*. (See pages 39–40.) The Inca slaves, the *yanacoma*, were slaves for life. Inca society was a closed society.

The long earlobes on this Inca figure show that he was one of the Inca nobility. Nobles were the only group of people allowed to wear very large ear disks.

RELIGION

The Incas believed that the world was made by Viracocha, the Creator God. He rose from the waters of Lake Titicaca and lived in Tiahuanaco where he created humans and taught them how to be civilized. He was also the father of the Sun and the Moon and was usually depicted as an old man with a beard. The Staff God at Chavin de Huantar and the Gateway God at Tiahuanaco (see pages 15 and 25)

A CLOSER LOOK

Like the Chimu before them, the Incas preserved the bodies of their rulers and allowed them to carry on "living" in their palaces after they died. The dead Sapa Inca sat on a golden stool and was served with food every day. A woman stood close by him to whisk away any flies that landed on his face, but most of his personal servants were ceremonially strangled when the Sapa Inca died, so that they could continue to look after him in the afterlife. The palace and all his possessions still belonged to him after death, and all his male descendants, apart from the next Sapa Inca, became his courtiers. The dead Sapa Incas were paraded through the streets of Cuzco during a ceremony known as the Festival of the Dead (right).

This stone carving of the god Viracocha is from Tiahuanaco. Also known as the Staff God, he would originally have held a staff in each hand.

A CLOSER LOOK
Inti became the most important Inca god during the reign of Pachacuti. He gave heat and light to the land and its people and helped their crops to grow and ripen in the fields. He was worshiped in temples throughout the empire, and many Inca religious festivals related to him.

are probably earlier versions of Viracocha.

Viracocha was invisible, but all the other Inca gods and goddesses could be seen or felt and were closely linked to looking after the land, the crops, and the animals upon which the people of the Inca Empire depended. The most important was Inti, the Sun god, from whom the Sapa Inca claimed to be descended. Like the Sapa Inca, he was married to his sister, Mama Quilla, who was the Moon goddess. The Inca people also worshiped Pacha Mama, who was the Earth goddess; Illapa, the god of thunder, rain and war; and Mama Cocha, the goddess of the sea who gave the Incas their fish.

INCA TEMPLES

There were temples of various sizes scattered throughout the Inca Empire. The most important was Coricancha, the temple of the Sun god in the center of Cuzco. Its walls were covered inside and out with sheets of beaten gold that was the symbol of Inti and was often known as "the sweat of the Sun." Inside the walls surrounding the temple was a garden containing models of corn plants and llamas, made from gold and silver. Beyond the garden was a courtyard surrounded by six buildings, each dedicated to a different god. They were also decorated with gold and silver. Inti himself was

represented by a huge disk of solid gold at the eastern end of the courtyard. The mummified bodies of the dead Sapa Incas were brought to visit him during important ceremonies.

PRIESTS AND THEIR HELPERS

The most important priest in the Inca religion was the High Priest. He lived in Cuzco and was usually a brother of the Sapa Inca. The priests who helped him were Inca nobles and, although they led a simple, religious life, they were very powerful and had great influence at court. Beneath them came thousands of other priests who lived and worked in temples throughout the empire. They were responsible for organizing worship, ceremonies, and sacrifices. They also acted as doctors and soothsayers, who predict the future. They were helped by other priests, Handmaidens of the Sun, (see box) and servants.

A silver model of a cornplant, similar to those in the garden at Coricancha.

HUACAS AND SACRIFICES

In addition to temples, there were many places, known as *huacas*, where people could pray and make

A CLOSER LOOK

When Inca girls were ten years old, they were divided into two groups. The most beautiful ones were sent to *mamacona* institutes, which were like convents, to be trained as Chosen Women, or *aqlla*. The rest remained in their villages and spent the next two years preparing for marriage. In a *mamacona* institute girls learned about the rituals of Inti worship, as well as how to cook and how to weave vicuña wool into finest cloth for the Sapa Inca and his Coya. After this training, the girls were split up again. Some became wives of high officials or even of the Sapa Inca himself, while a few were sacrificed to the gods. Most became Handmaidens of the Sun and were sent to help the priests in the temples. Besides assisting in ceremonies, they also prepared special foods and drinks for festivals.

This mamacona *figure is made from silver.*

Inca children probably played with dolls made from reeds and cotton, like this one. Some of these dolls were left as sacrifices at huacas.

sacrifices as other Andean peoples had done before them. *Huacas* were places, such as rocks, springs, and caves, where local ancestor spirits were thought to dwell. Each *huaca* was considered to have special powers, and the Incas made offerings to them when they needed help. These offerings varied according to the importance of the *huaca*, the importance of the request, and the wealth of the one who is asking for something. The poorest person might offer a few eyelashes or a little beer, while a rich person might leave a gold ornament or a fine garment. At the most powerful *huacas*, sacrifices of guinea pigs and llamas were made. In times of war, severe drought, or earthquakes, people were also sacrificed.

A CLOSER LOOK

In the harsh climate of Peru, people needed to work together in order to survive. Long before the Incas came to power, many people had organized themselves into large family groups, or *ayllus*. The Incas took this idea and used it as a way of arranging their empire. *Ayllus* varied in size, from the smallest farming village to the city of Cuzco itself, but each one looked after its own members and was responsible for farming its own land.

EVERYDAY LIFE FOR THE PEASANTS

Within each *ayllu*, everyone knew what they were expected to do, since both men and women were divided into ten categories by their age. Most of the work was done by those between 16 and 60 years old, but even children had to start learning useful skills once they reached the age of two, and old people were also expected to help in the house and in the fields whenever they could. Women were married at the age of 12. After that their tasks included cooking, spinning, weaving, and looking after the children, while men had to pay the public duty tax, or *mit'a*, as well as making sure they grew enough crops to feed their family and pay their taxes to the Sapa Inca and to the Sun God.

Houses for most people were built of stone or adobe bricks and had thatched roofs. They were one story high and had no real furniture. However, what people ate and how they lived depended on where they lived in the empire. Communities on the coast relied on fishing for their main food supply, while people in the river valleys grew corn, squash, tomatoes, peanuts, beans, peppers, and cassava, and kept guinea pigs and ducks for their meat. They also grew cotton that was spun and woven into cloth for their clothes. In the colder highlands, *quinoa*, a grain, and white and sweet potatoes were the main food crops, while herds of llamas and alpacas occasionally provided meat as well as wool for clothing and blankets. People also grew the coca plant and chewed its leaves to help them work at high altitudes.

A pottery model of village houses. Buildings were often constructed as closely together as possible in order not to take up too much valuable farmland.

Although it was a hard life, the year was broken up by many religious festivals at which there was often dancing—and plenty of celebrating! If people were too old or ill to work, they were looked after by other members of the *ayllu*, while the state provided them with the food and clothing they needed from what had been collected as taxes.

Science and Technology

When the Spaniards arrived in Peru in 1532, they found a country in which horses and wheeled vehicles were unknown, and the skill of working with iron was only just beginning to develop. As the horse, the wheel, and ironworking had been essential to the growth of civilizations in much of Europe for almost 2,000 years, the Spaniards thought that the Incas were backward and made no attempt to understand the people or the land they lived in. However, wheeled vehicles would have made very little progress on the steep slopes of the Andes, even if there had been horses to pull them. The Incas and earlier civilizations in Peru already had tools and weapons that met their needs very well. In addition, the Incas had developed an efficient system of communication. They knew how to construct large buildings that could withstand earthquakes. Their "doctors" performed brain operations and blood transfusions. Perhaps most important, their farmers were skilled at successfully growing crops in the harshest deserts and on steep mountain slopes.

Farming

A closer look

To make the rain start again in October, Inca priests sometimes performed a ritual in which special black llamas were starved until they cried with hunger and thirst. The farmers believed that this crying would make Illapa, the rain god, take pity on the animals and send the rains to quench their thirst.

All the civilizations of ancient Peru relied on farmers to fully use the many different types of terrains and climate across the region, and grow enough food to sustain the whole population. In the coastal desert, where almost no rain fell, farmers made irrigation channels to direct water to the fields from the rivers that flowed from the

Andes to the ocean. With no natural shelter from the heat of the sun or the drying wind, water soon evaporated if it flowed in the open air. To prevent this from happening, many channels were covered with flat stones and then with soil.

In the mountains there was plenty of rain. But it did not fall all year round, so farmers built stone reservoirs to store rainwater. They also made more flat land available for farming by constructing terraces on the steep mountain slopes. This involved building long stone walls along the contour of the mountainside and then bringing soil up from the valley and piling it behind each wall. The soil was

Land terraced for agriculture at Pisac, above the valley of the Vilcanota River.

A CLOSER LOOK

High in the Andes the main crop was potatoes of various kinds. After they had been harvested, the potatoes were left outside at night where they quickly froze in the subzero temperatures. They were then dried in the hot sun to produce a food called *chunu* that could be stored and eaten when fresh food was scarce. Strips of meat called *charki* were also preserved in this way for later use.

A CLOSER LOOK
Much of the gold used by the peoples of ancient Peru came from streams and rivers. It was found as nuggets or tiny specks mixed in with the gravel on the riverbed. The gold was heated until it turned to liquid. This required a temperature of about 3,600° F (2,000° C), which the metalworkers achieved by blowing through tubes into a pan filled with burning charcoal. A clay pot or crucible containing the ore was placed directly into the fire, and the molten gold collected at the bottom of it. It was then poured into molds to form ingots of pure gold before being used to make beautiful ornaments or jewelry.

leveled off to give a flat surface on which to grow crops. To keep the soil fertile, manure was spread on it, but the best fertilizer of all was thought to be the droppings of seabirds. During the dry season, which lasted from June to September in the mountains, the terraces were irrigated with water brought in channels from the reservoirs.

TOOLS AND WEAPONS

From before Chavin times, people made both tools and weapons from stone, wood, and animal bone. They used a kind of volcanic glass, called obsidian, to make knife blades with a cutting edge as sharp as steel. They shaped other stones into axheads and hammerheads that could be held in the hand or attached to wooden handles. Digging sticks made from wood were used to turn the soil before planting seeds. For attack and defense, people used heavy wooden clubs, some of which were tipped with stone or bronze for stabbing as well as hitting. Other weapons included wooden lances and spears, and bows and arrows that were used for hunting.

BUILDING TECHNIQUES

In the desert along the coast, people constructed their houses and other buildings from adobe bricks. These buildings lasted well in areas where there was very little rainfall, but they would have soon broken apart in the heavy rain and snow that fell in the mountains. People in the highlands used stone to construct their buildings. Although they had no iron tools, no explosives, and no lifting equipment, they were able to cut and move stones weighing up to 100 tons. No one is certain how they did this, but it is thought that stonemasons looked for natural

cracks in the stone in a quarry and then forced wooden wedges into them. The wood was then soaked with water until it expanded and made the crack wider and deeper. This process was repeated until it was possible to free the block of stone with the help of wood or bronze crowbars and stone hammers. Ropes were fastened around the stone, and it was dragged to the building site by large teams of men. There it was cut into the required size with stone hammers and axes.

Some Inca walls still stand today in the former capital of Cuzco.

The great skill of Tiahuanacan and Inca building, however, was in the shaping of the stone. Again this was done with stone hammers and possibly also bronze chisels. No two stones were ever quite the same size and shape. The stones had many faces and sometimes as many as 30 corners, but they all interlocked perfectly with each other, and no mortar was needed to hold the walls together. This precise fit allowed many of these structures to survive earthquakes with very little damage.

A paved Inca road near Intipunku in the Andes. Farmers built and maintained the roads as part of their labor tax.

ROADS

Like the Chimu before them, the Incas built a vast system of roads to link all parts of their empire. The two most important roads ran the full length of the empire, one through the mountains and the other across the coastal desert. The roads were used mainly by the emperor's messengers and by people transporting goods. Their construction varied depending upon the terrain, but they were usually paved with stone. A mixture of clay, pebbles, and crushed corn leaves was often used to smooth out rough areas. The Incas built the roads in as straight a line as possible, with flights of steps on the steepest slopes.

Various kinds of bridges were built to cross the rivers, depending on the river's width. Solid bridges made from wooden planks crossed small streams and very narrow rivers. If a river was wide, slow-flowing, and between low banks, reed boats might be tied together to create a pontoon bridge. Deep valleys were crossed by suspension bridges that workers from the nearest *ayllus* made and maintained. (See box below).

A CLOSER LOOK

Suspension bridges were usually made from rope. Each household in the *ayllu* had to make its share from the dry flower stalks of *q'oya* grass. The women spun a length of two-ply rope with their hands until it was about as thick as a finger. The men then stretched these ropes out in bundles and twisted them into six cables, each about 8 inches (20 cm) centimeters in diameter. Each cable was braided to stop it from untwisting. A stone pillar was built at either side of the valley, and the first cable was taken across and firmly attached at each end. Three more were stretched alongside it to make the bottom of the bridge, then the other two were added as handrails. The four bottom cables were lashed together to make a flat platform on which planks of wood could be laid for a walkway. Finally, the two handrails were lashed to the bottom to hold the bridge together.

This modern suspension bridge over the Pampas River was made in just the same way as the Inca bridges.

MEDICINE

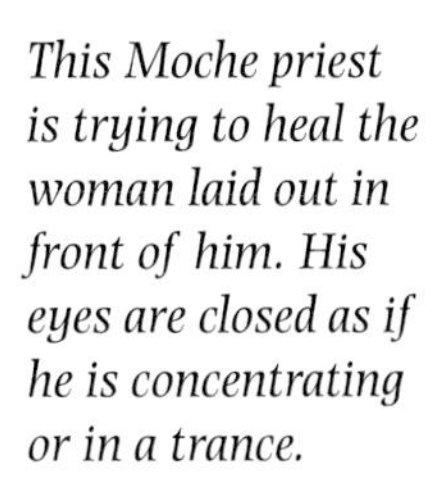

This Moche priest is trying to heal the woman laid out in front of him. His eyes are closed as if he is concentrating or in a trance.

By Inca times, the people of Peru, their doctors, and healers had knowledge of many different remedies for injuries and illnesses. The leaves of the coca plant were chewed to ease pain, stop hunger pangs, and help people cope with the harsh climate and high altitude. Leaves of the cassava plant were boiled to make a potion that was good for aching joints. A special type of clay was eaten to try to cure gout, and a mineral called jasper was crushed and used to stop bleeding. People also used quinine as a cure for fevers and to heal wounds. Many of these medicines were obtained from official chemists, known as *hampi camayoc*. Some were also obtained from people called *collahuaya*, who were shamans, or medical specialists. They also supplied lucky charms that were worn to ward off disease.

In the *ayllus*, Inca priests often acted as surgeons. They anesthetized their patients with coca leaves or *chicha* (beer) and operated on them with knives made from gold, silver, copper, obsidian, or flint. They knew how to amputate crushed limbs, set broken bones, pull out teeth, and even give blood transfusions.

A CLOSER LOOK

Archaeologists in Peru have found many skulls that have been carefully cut open. Since some of the holes show signs of healing, the patients obviously survived the surgery, but nobody knows why it was done. It might have been to relieve pressure on the brain after a blow to the head, or to release the evil spirits that were thought to possess some people.

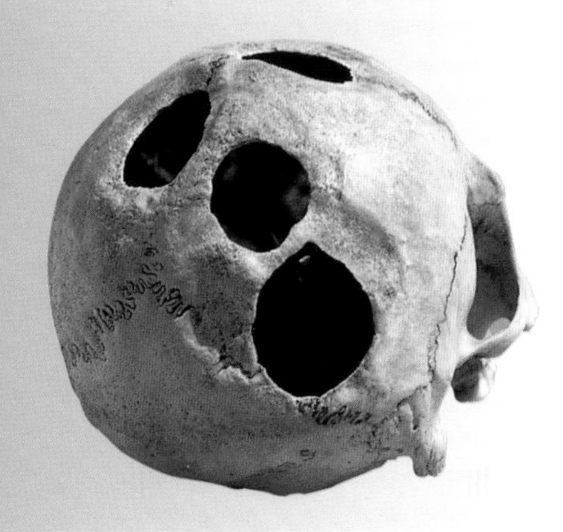

This skull has been cut open at least four times.

ASTRONOMY AND CALENDARS

Because the peoples of Peru depended on farming to survive, they needed some means of marking the passing of the seasons, so that they could plow their fields and plant their seeds at the correct times. The Inca emperor, Pachacuti, drew up a calendar of 12 months, each divided into 30 days. Simple observatories were also built for the priests to watch the movements of the Sun and the planets. Some consisted of just a single stone pillar whose shadow would allow the priest to measure the movement of the Sun. But others had several pillars with pierced disks on top that the Sun's rays would pass through at different times of year.

A CLOSER LOOK

The single stone pillar for measuring the movement of the Sun was possibly known as an Inti Huatana. This means "the post where the Sun is tied." In the winter the Incas watched its shadow carefully, waiting for the moment when the Sun reached the solstice and was at the farthest point from the Inca lands. Religious ceremonies then took place to encourage the Sun to come back and warm the Inca lands once more. In their determination to wipe out all traces of the Inca religion, the Spaniards destroyed every Inti Huatana they found.

The Spaniards never found the Inca stronghold of Machu Picchu—and so its Inti Huatana survived.

ARTS AND CRAFTS

Many Inca artifacts were stolen or destroyed by the Spaniards in the 16th century, and others have been stolen by grave-robbers in more recent times. Even so, enough survive to show us that the Incas and their predecessors were skilled potters, stonemasons, and metalworkers. Many items were produced for everyday use, but the most ornate were probably made especially to be buried with the dead, either to show the person's importance in this life or as offerings to the gods.

SHARED IMAGES

From Chavin times to the defeat of the Inca Empire, all the peoples of Peru used similar images to decorate their pottery and textiles, carvings, and metalwork. These images were based on the natural world and on religious ideas. They included jaguars, condors, snakes, eagles, caimans, crocodiles, frogs, and humans, and many strange creatures that were made up of the features of two or three different animals or humans. There were also many different versions of the Staff God. (See page 15.) Some designs from the coastal areas show mountain scenes, while some designs from the mountain areas show the ocean and off-shore islands, confirming that the various civilizations knew about each other's territory from early times. However, although the same images reappear, they were depicted in different ways at different times. Sometimes they looked realistic, at other times they had geometric shapes or lengthened arms and legs, making them harder to recognize.

POTTERY

This Moche pot is in the shape of an imaginary creature with a snake's body, the head of a deer, and the teeth of a large cat.

Pottery was first made in Peru around 2000 B.C. Before that date, plant gourds were used as containers for storage and as cups and bowls. But after that date, corn became an increasingly important crop. Corn needed to be cooked in pots so, as this knowledge spread, pottery gradually replaced gourds in everyday use.

Early pottery was either plain or very simply decorated, but by Chavin times designs were carved in low relief or painted onto the pots. The Paracas people cut their designs into the clay, as did the early Nazca people. Later Nazca pottery has multicolored designs, and often shows the image of the Strangler, a mythological creature with a long, pointed tongue. Moche pottery was often shaped to represent people, animals, and plants. Some pots represented a single human face, but others showed several different figures in action, including battle scenes and hunting scenes, mothers and their children, healers and priests at work, and the punishment of criminals and prisoners of war.

The man on this Inca pot is carrying a large waterpot on his back.

Pottery from Tiahuanaco, as early as A.D. 200, and Huari, too, was painted in different colors. Chimu pottery was largely mass-produced and mainly black in color. But, the Incas made a full range of items, from painted vases and bowls, to figures of people, and large, patterned waterpots, known as *aryballos*, that were designed so that the water did

A CLOSER LOOK
Of all the goods produced in the Inca Empire, one-third was set aside for the Sapa Inca, and one-third for the Sun God. Only the remaining third could be traded. There was no system of money, so that everything was exchanged for something of equal value. People from the highlands exchanged wool, dried meat, and dried potatoes for salt, fish, fruit, cotton, beans, and corn from the coast and the lowlands, and for feathers, dyes, and drugs from the rain forests. These items were also traded in exchange for pottery and textiles.

not spill out when the the pot was being carried on someone's back.

All these pots were made without the aid of a fast-spinning potter's wheel. Sometimes the shape was achieved by coiling long strips of clay on top of each other, but some pots were molded in the hand from a ball of clay. Many pots with a person's image were made in two halves, by smoothing clay inside two molds, then removing it just before it dried out and sticking the two parts together. When the pot had been shaped, it was dried in the sun, then painted, and finally fired to harden it.

TEXTILES

In ancient Peru, the finest textiles were valued more highly than gold. Textiles were often buried with the dead, not just as clothing, but also as beautifully patterned lengths of cloth to wrap around the mummified body. From the Chavin civilization to that of the Incas, cotton and wool from the backs of alpaca and vicuña were spun and woven into good-quality cloth, while wool from llamas was used for items such as ropes and rough blankets.

Only an Inca of high status would have been allowed to wear a richly decorated tunic such as this one from the south coast of Peru.

Textile patterns were created in many different ways. Patterns were woven on the loom by using yarns of different colors. Plain cloth could also be tie-dyed or have patterns painted on it. The most spectacular designs, however, were those made by the Paracas people for use as burial cloths. (See page 8.) These cloths had alternating plain and embroidered squares, with no two patterns ever being exactly the same. They showed warriors holding severed heads, priests flying in trances, animals and plants, and people dressed as animals. Almost 200 different colors have been counted in the embroidery that was done with needles made from bone or wood. It has been estimated that each cloth took up to 30 years to complete. These patterns probably related to the dead person's status in life, but other, simpler patterns were also used to distinguish the costumes worn by people from each village or *ayllu*.

A CLOSER LOOK
Most of the dyes for cloth were made from the roots, leaves, or flowers of many different plants, but bright red was obtained from the bodies of cochineal insects that had been dried and crushed.

Featherwork garments were worn only for special festivals and ceremonies. Besides the human figure in the center, this one is patterned with birds and fish.

FEATHERWORK

Cloaks, *ruanas* (ponchos), and tunics for wealthy nobles and rulers were sometimes decorated with patterns made from brightly colored feathers. The feathers were taken from wild birds caught in the Amazon rain forests. The garment itself was made from woven cloth with the quills of the feathers pushed through from front to back and carefully attached. Thousands of feathers were needed for just one garment. Feathers were also used to make headdresses for nobles and to make fans (see page 36) and whisks to cool the face, or flick flies and insects away.

A CLOSER LOOK

From Chavin times, gold jewelry was worn as a sign of a person's social status. It was made into armlets and bracelets, necklaces, and pendants. It was also made into ear disks that were mainly worn by noblemen and priests. These ear disks were often decorated with inlaid patterns made from pieces of turquoise or shell, or from colored feathers. Men had their ears pierced when they were quite young and wore bigger and bigger disks in the hole to stretch it, until it was big enough to push an egg through!

METALWORK

Gold was used in Peru for ornaments and jewelry from at least Chavin times. At first, people hammered it into sheets that could be cut or bent into the required shape and decorated with embossed, or raised, patterns. By Chimu times, however, many more metalworking skills had been mastered. Chimu goldsmiths knew how to weld pieces of gold together, shape cups and dishes around wooden templates, make inlaid and filigree patterns, fix a layer of gold plating on to copper objects and create beautiful ornaments using the lost-wax method of casting metal. They also used tiny plates of gold to decorate clothes and bags for

Chimu goldsmiths made this mask by beating pieces of gold into shape. Two snarling, catlike creatures hang upside down from the ax shaped headdress.

the very rich. When the Incas conquered the Chimu, they were so impressed with Chimu workmanship that they took the best goldsmiths from Chan Chan to Cuzco to work for the emperor.

MUSIC AND DANCE

Throughout the Inca year, there were many festivals. Some were linked to farming, celebrating a plentiful harvest or a successful sowing of seeds. Others were religious festivals or marked events in the lives of the people in the *ayllus*, such as coming-of-age or marriage ceremonies. Food and drink played an important part at these celebrations, as well as music. Archaeologists have found the remains of panpipes, flutes, drums, and even a clay trumpet from Inca times and earlier. A 17th-century drawing by Poma de Ayala shows women singing and beating drums, while the men are dressed as birds and getting ready to dance.

This pottery bottle shows a man playing a tune on the panpipes.

STORYTELLING AND HISTORY

With no written language, the peoples of ancient Peru learned stories and history by heart and passed them from one generation to the next by word of mouth. In Inca times, when the Sapa Inca died, a council of nobles met and decided which parts of his life should be remembered. These were recorded on *quipus* (see page 30), and people known as rememberers also learned what to say about the dead ruler. Nearly all of this oral history and information was lost, however, when most of the *quipus* were destroyed by the Spanish invaders.

Civil War and the Defeat of the Incas

Inca history was eventually written down by the Spaniards after the conquest of the Inca Empire. They tell us that in 1525, while the Sapa Inca Huayna Capac was trying to extend his empire northward, he was told of an epidemic that was sweeping through Cuzco and the surrounding area. He quickly turned south and tried to deal with the problem, but reached only as far as present-day Quito before falling ill himself. No one today is sure what the epidemic was, but it seems likely to have been either smallpox or measles. Both these diseases were introduced to South America by the Spaniards who settled around La Plata on the east coast. These diseases were probably brought to the Andes area by people who traded with the Spaniards. Since the native peoples had not been exposed to these diseases before, they had no natural resistance to them, and large numbers died.

Huayna Capac's successors

Huayna Capac's death was sudden and unexpected. As a result, he did not have time to name his successor properly. By tradition it should have been his son by the Coya, but she had no children. In such a case, the Sapa Inca was supposed to choose his successor with the help of divine approval. Huayna Capac had chosen Ninan Cuyuchi who was with him, but Huayna Capac died before the priest could perform the ceremony

A closer look

When the Sapa Inca did not have a son by his sister (the Coya), he needed to choose one of his other sons to be Sapa Inca after him. Once he had made his choice, he asked his priest to sacrifice a llama and remove its lungs. A sign on the lungs would show whether the gods approved of the Sapa Inca's choice or not. If they did not, then another son was chosen and the ceremony was repeated.

of approval, and Ninan Cuyuchi died shortly afterward. Huascar, another son who was in Cuzco at the time, was Huayna Capac's next choice. The priest in Quito decided to name him as the next Sapa Inca without any ceremony of approval. This angered Atahuallpa, Huascar's half-brother, who was in Quito with Huayna Capac and his army. Huascar demanded that Atahuallpa return to Cuzco, but Atahuallpa refused. An official was then sent to see him, but Atahuallpa's response was to kill him and have a drum made out of his skin. When the drum was sent to Huascar, civil war broke out between the two brothers and their supporters.

The war lasted until April 1532, when Huascar's army was finally defeated, and Huascar himself was taken prisoner. At that time Atahuallpa was at a town called Cajamarca, and he ordered Huascar to be brought to him there. Atahuallpa was now Sapa Inca, but his reign was destined to be a short one.

THE SPANIARDS ARRIVE

Since Christopher Columbus had first sailed to the West Indies in 1492, the Spaniards had gradually been building an empire in what they called the "New World." The Spanish took control of Mexico in 1521. During the next ten years, groups of adventurers set off both north and south in search of gold and other treasures. One of these groups, led by Francisco Pizarro, landed at Tumbes on the north coast of Peru early in 1532. Pizarro led fewer than 200 men, most of whom were soldiers. They had

A CLOSER LOOK

Francisco Pizarro was born in Spain around 1478 and went to the Spanish colony of Hispaniola, now Haiti and the Dominican Republic, in 1502. He started his explorations of South America in 1510. From 1519 to 1523 he was mayor of Panama, a town that had been founded by the Spaniards. Over the next nine years, he went on several more expeditions along the west coast of the continent. On one of these, he crossed the equator and met a raft traveling from Peru with a cargo of embroidered cloth and precious metals. He must have also heard that the Inca Empire was being torn apart by civil war and would be relatively easy to conquer.

guns and wore armor, and about a third of them were on horseback. By the end of the year, the Inca Empire would be under their control.

THE MEETING AT CAJAMARCA

After they had defeated Huascar, Atahuallpa's soldiers went to join their leader in a camp at Cajamarca. There they heard stories about the strangers who had landed on the coast and were now heading toward them. Atahuallpa was curious but not afraid, since he had around 50,000 men with him. When Pizarro and his soldiers arrived in Cajamarca, they invited Atahuallpa to go and meet them on November 16, 1532. Atahuallpa accepted the invitation. His attendants carried him to the meeting on a golden litter, and his bodyguard of around 6,000 men went too. Atahuallpa was expecting a peaceful meeting, but Pizarro and his men had prepared an ambush.

Poma de Ayala drew this picture of Atahuallpa and Pizarro at Cajamarca almost 90 years after the meeting took place.

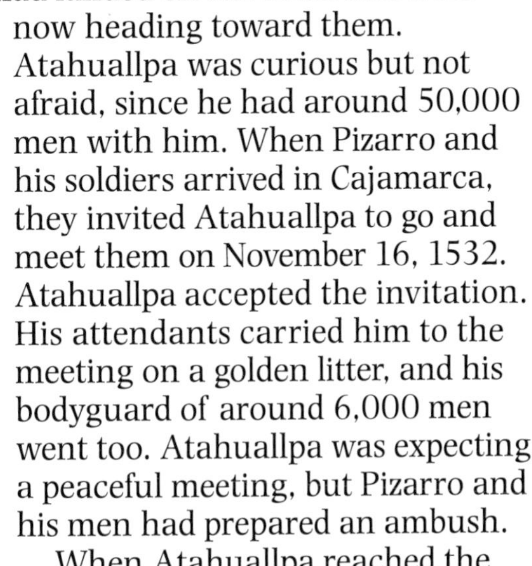

When Atahuallpa reached the main square of Cajamarca, a Spanish priest stepped forward and started to preach to him, offering him a Bible. Atahuallpa, who had never seen a book before, looked at it carefully and, then, threw it down because it meant nothing to him. The Spaniards took this as a signal to attack and began shooting at the unarmed Incas. Many of them were killed, and Atahuallpa was taken prisoner.

THE DEATH OF ATAHUALLPA

Realizing that the Spaniards were interested in gold, Atahuallpa offered them a room filled with gold objects in exchange for his freedom. Pizarro agreed, but, once the room was full, he took the treasure and still kept Atahuallpa in prison. While he was held captive, Atahuallpa ordered the execution of his rival, Huascar, to prevent the Spaniards from making him Sapa Inca in Atahuallpa's place. Pizarro used this as an excuse to charge Atahuallpa with murder. The Sapa Inca was found guilty and sentenced to be burned to death. Believing that the destruction of his body would prevent him from living again after his death, Atahuallpa finally agreed to accept Christianity in exchange for the promise that he would be strangled to death rather than burned. He was baptized on August 29, 1533, and executed on the same day.

SPANISH RULE

Having been strictly ruled by the Sapa Inca, the people did not know what to do when Atahuallpa was dead. Though some tried to resist the Spaniards, their weapons were no match for guns and cannons, and they were eventually defeated. Their temples were destroyed, and their treasures were stolen.

A CLOSER LOOK

After the death of Atahuallpa, the Spaniards put another of Huayna Capac's sons on the throne as Sapa Inca. His name was Manco Inca, but he was a puppet ruler and had to do what the Spaniards told him. He managed to escape to a remote area called Vitcos, where he set up a small but independent Inca state with its capital at Vilcabamba. This state survived until 1572. Vilcabamba was the city that archaeologist Hiram Bingham was looking for in 1911, when he discovered the ruins of Machu Picchu.

Manco Inca sitting on his throne surrounded by his warriors, as drawn by Poma de Ayala in 1620.

The Christian church of Santa Domingo now stands on the site of Coricancha in Cuzco, but the walls of the old Inca shrine can still be seen in the foreground.

Missionaries arrived from Spain to convert them to Christianity, and a monastery was built on the site of Coricancha. By 1535 the Spaniards had complete control of Peru. They turned many of its people into slaves and forced them to work in the fields and in the gold and silver mines. The Spaniards did not understand the irrigation systems and let them fall into ruin. The crops failed, and soon people began to starve to death. Many more were killed by diseases brought from Europe. The Inca people and their civilization were almost wiped out. But in remote parts, some of the old gods and the old traditions were remembered and managed to survive until the 19th century, when the country regained its independence. Though Spanish remains the main language in Peru, and Christianity is the country's main religion, some of the Inca ways are still a part of life today. One example is Festival of Inti Raymi that celebrates the return of the Sun after the winter solstice.

A CLOSER LOOK

In 1535, Francisco Pizarro founded the city of Lima as the new capital of Peru, and Cuzco lost its earlier importance. Because of his ruthlessness, Pizarro had many enemies among the Spaniards, and in June 1541 they joined forces and attacked his palace in Lima. Pizarro was killed, but in 1542, the conquistadores chose his half-brother, Gonzalo Pizarro, as the new governor of Peru.

TIMELINE

Note: The earliest accurate date in the history of Peru is 1438 when Pachacuti Inca Yupanqui came to the throne. All the dates before this are based on archaeological evidence, and so they are approximate, rather than exact.

B.C.

10,000	People are living in Peru by this date.
8000	Attempts are made to cultivate some plants in the fertile valleys.
6000	Potatoes are cultivated in the highlands.
3000	The first people start to settle on the coast.
2500	People start to settle in the river valleys and in the highlands.
2300	Large-scale building projects start in the river valleys.
2000	Cultivation of corn starts, and pottery begins to appear.
1700	The first large ceremonial centers are built.
1000	People start to settle around Tiahuanaco.
900	Possible start of the Chavin civilization
850	Work begins on the temple complex at Chavin de Huantar.
600	Probable start of the Paracas civilization
200	Collapse of the Chavin civilization and start of the Nazca civilization

A.D.

1	Start of the Moche civilization
175	Collapse of the Paracas civilization
300	The Lord of Sipan is buried.
500	The Tiahuanacan civilization starts to expand.
600	The start of the Huari civilization
800	The Nazca and Moche civilizations have collapsed by this date.
900	By this date the Huari civilization has collapsed, and Huari has been abandoned.
1000	Start of the Chimu civilization
1100	The Tiahuanacan civilization has collapsed by this date.
1200	Construction of the Chimu capital, Chan Chan, begins. Manco Capac, the first Inca emperor, takes his people to Cuzco and builds his capital city there.
1438	Pachacuti Inca Yupanqui becomes Sapa Inca and greatly expands the Inca Empire.
1471	Topa Inca Yupanqui becomes Sapa Inca, and the expansion continues.
1476	The Incas defeat the Chimu and make their lands part of the Inca Empire.
1491	Huayna Capac becomes Sapa Inca.
1525	The Inca Empire is at its greatest extent when Huayna Capac dies.
1532	In April, Atahuallpa defeats his half-brother Huascar and becomes Sapa Inca. The Spaniards, led by Francisco Pizarro, land at Tumbes in northern Peru. In November, Pizarro tricks Atahuallpa and takes him prisoner.
1533	Atahuallpa is executed by the Spaniards on August 29. The Spaniards make Manco Inca the new Sapa Inca.
1535	Francisco Pizarro founds Lima as the new capital of Peru.
1537	Manco Inca escapes to Vilcabamba and sets up an independent Inca state.
1541	Francisco Pizarro is killed by his enemies.
1572	Tupac Amaru, one of Manco Inca's sons, becomes the last Sapa Inca. He is captured by the Spaniards and executed. The Inca Empire comes to an end.

Glossary

adobe – bricks made from clay and dried in the sun.
altiplano – a bleak area of high grassland in the Lake Titicaca region of the Andes.
ayllu – a social group based on an extended family structure. It could be as small as a village or as large as a city.
bullion – gold and silver in bars and ingots.
caiman – an animal related to the alligator.
camelid – a member of the camel family. In South America these include the vicuña, llama, alpaca, and guanaco.
cassava – a plant. Its roots can be made into a type of flour.
colony – a group of people who settle in a foreign country.
conquistadores – the Spaniards who conquered Mexico and Peru in the 16th century.
El Niño – the name given to unusually warm ocean conditions that affect weather over much of the Pacific Ocean every 4 to 12 years. El Niño can cause devastating storms and floods.
filigree – fine metalwork that is similar to lace.
hallucinogenic – describes substances such as drugs that cause hallucinations.
huaca – shrines at rocks, springs, or caves where people left offerings and made sacrifices.
litter – a seat on poles on which the Sapa Inca was carried by his servants.
mit'a – tax paid with manual labor.
mummies – bodies that have been preserved after death by drying .
oracle – a place where the gods can be asked to give advice or predict the future.
pontoon – a bridge made by fastening boats together and sometimes placing planks across them to make a walkway.
puna – high, treeless grassland in the Andes.
puppet ruler – someone who is given the title of ruler with no power, while someone else is really in control.
Quechua – the language spoken by the Incas, and their ancestors.
quinine – a drug from the bark of the cinchona tree used to cure fevers.
quinoa – a high-protein grain that grows at high altitudes.
quipu – a collection of knotted strings used by the Incas for recording numbers and other information. A memory device for oral history.
***ruana* (poncho)** – a cloak made of an oblong piece of cloth with a hole in the middle for the head to go through.
Sapa Inca – "Sole Ruler," the emperor of the Incas.
shaman – a ritual specialist who reads omens, predicts the future, and performs ceremonies.
smelting – obtaining metal from ore by means of heating it.
solstice – the day of the year when the sun is directly overhead at either the Tropic of Cancer or the Tropic of Capricorn.
trapezoid – a four-sided figure, like a triangle with the top cut off.
tribute – a set amount of goods given by conquered people to their new rulers, usually in exchange for peace and protection.
trophy head – the head of an enemy taken in battle and kept as proof of victory.

Further Reading

*Barber, Nicola. *The Search for Gold*, "Treasure Hunters" series. Raintree Steck-Vaughn, Austin, 1998

*Cameron, Ian. *Kingdom of the Sun Gods: A History of the Andes and Their People*. Facts on File, New York, 1990

Cobo, Bernabe, John H. Rowe, and Roland Hamilton. *History of the Inca Empire*. University of Texas Press, Austin, 1983

Collier, R. Rosaldo and J. Wirth. *The Inca and Aztec States 1400–1800*. Academic Press, New York, 1982

*Gonzales, Christina. *Inca Civilizations*. Children's Press, Danbury, 1993

*Hoobler, Dorothy, and Tom Hoobler. *The Fact or Fiction Files: Lost Civilizations*. Walker and Company, New York, 1992

Jennings, Jesse D., ed. *Ancient South Americans*. Freeman, San Francisco, 1983

*Kendall, Sarita H. *The Incas*, "World of the Past" series. Simon & Schuster Childrens, Englewood Cliffs, 1992

Lumbraras, Luis. *The People and Cultures of Ancient Peru*. Smithsonian Institution, Washington, D.C., 1974

Mosely, Michael E. *The Incas and Their Ancestors: The Archaeology of Peru*. Thames and Hudson, New York, 1992

*Odijk, Pamela. *The Incas*, "Ancient World" series. Silver Burdett Press, Parsippany, 1990

*Sayer, Chloë. *The Incas*, "Ancient World" series. Raintree Steck-Vaughn, Austin, 1998

*Steele, Philip. *The Incas and Machu Picchu*, "Hidden Worlds" series. Silver Burdett Press, Parsippany, 1993

*Indicates this is a Young Adult book.

INDEX